A FREE GI

Attract Money Forever will deepen your understanding of metaphysics and mind-power principles as they relate to attracting money, manifesting abundance, and governing material reality. You'll learn how to use time-tested, time-honored, practical, and spiritual techniques to be more prosperous and improve your life in astounding and meaningful ways. Visit jamesgoijr.com/subscriber-page.html for your free download copy of this amazing book and to receive James's free monthly *Mind Power & Money Ezine*.

LIGHT
VS.
DARKNESS

Books by James Goi Jr.

How to Attract Money Using Mind Power
Attract Money Forever
Ten Metaphysical Secrets of Manifesting Money
Advanced Manifesting Made Easy
Aware Power Functioning
The God Function
The Supernatural Power of Thought
Ten Spiritual Secrets of Dead People
Ten Spiritual Secrets of Divine Order
Ten Spiritual Secrets of Thought Power
Self-Defense Techniques and How to Win a Street Fight
The Healing Power of the Light
Spirituality and Metaphysics
Unconditional Love Demystified
Spiritual Power Demystified
Intuition Demystified
Message from the Presence
The True Nature of Reality
Reincarnation and Karma
Vibration and Frequency
Spiritual Understanding
Spiritual Advancement
Spiritual Knowledge
Spiritual Wisdom
Success Consciousness
Higher Consciousness
Light vs. Darkness
The New Normal
My Song Lyrics (multiple volumes)
JGJ Thoughts, Vol. 1

Note

James continues to write new books.
To see the current list, visit his author page at Amazon.com

LIGHT
VS.
DARKNESS

A Spiritual Inquiry into Reality and Illusion

JAMES GOI JR.

JGJ
JAMES GOI JR.
LA MESA, CALIFORNIA

Copyright © 2022 by James Goi Jr.

All rights reserved. Brief passages of this book may be used in reviews but except as allowed by United States and international copyright law, no part of this book may be reproduced or transmitted in any form or by any means, electronic, mechanical, magnetic, photographic including photocopying, recording, or by any information storage and retrieval system without prior written permission of the publisher. No patent liability is assumed with respect to the use of the information contained herein, and the publisher and author assume no responsibility for errors, inaccuracies, omissions, or inconsistencies.

The information contained in this book is intended to be educational and not prescriptive, and is not meant to replace consultation with professionals in any field. Always seek professional help and guidance when needed.

ISBN:
978-1-68347-086-1 (Trade Paperback)
978-1-68347-087-8 (Kindle)
978-1-68347-088-5 (epub)

Published by:
James Goi Jr.
P.O. Box 563
La Mesa, CA, 91944
www.jamesgoijr.com

TRADEMARK NOTICE: The Attract Money Guru™ and Books to Awaken, Uplift, and Empower™ are trademarks of James Goi Jr.

CONTENTS

Preface

1. Spiritual Light 1
2. Spiritual Darkness 3
3. Embracing the Light 5
4. Reality and Illusion 7
5. Living in Reality 9
6. Contemplation 11
7. Transcending Belief 13
8. Turn Within 15
9. Consciousness 17
10. Subjective Reality 19
11. The Perceiver 21
12. Your True Self 23
13. The Dreamer 25
14. Beyond Form 27
Afterword 29
About the Author 31
Special Acknowledgement 35
Further Reading 39

PREFACE

As I sat down to write this book, it was 7:42 a.m. US Pacific Time on Monday, 3/21/22. I had no idea when I woke up that morning that I would be starting a new book, much less what the subject of that book would be. But as you might know, I never let such things keep me from writing a book whose time has come.

I had a little conversation with Kathy that morning and, well, one thing must have led to another because by the end of that conversation I knew the title of this book and that I would begin my writing on that day.

A little while later I made my way to my computer, and wrote the first four chapters. I wrote on and off for the next few days, and finished the first draft of this book early on Friday morning, 3/25/22. I had no direction at all while writing. Except for the second chapter, I did not know what the subject of the next chapter would be until I was finishing up the chapter I was working on. Now that I've pointed that out to you, I think you will be able to see what I mean.

Quite a while back, the idea came to me to write a book about, well, basically what this book turned out to be. Though, as usual, I had no idea what the specifics would be. Then I forgot all about it. Then early that Monday morning I was reminded of it again. Enjoy.

1
Spiritual Light

The Light we are discussing in this book is spiritual Light, not physical light. And I will capitalize the word as a reminder of that distinction, and out of respect.

But trying to fit spiritual Light into physical words can be likened to, say, trying to stuff the sun into your pocket. Try as you might, you're just not going to be able to do it. Now having gotten that out of the way, I will just proceed on and do the best I can do. And strictly speaking, I will not even try to *define* spiritual Light. The best I can hope to do, I guess, is to just say some things about it using the words I come up with.

So, what *can* I say about Light? Well, for starters, the word *Light* seems to denote something that is universal, fundamental, spiritual, divine, and good. Light embodies intelligence, knowledge, wisdom, grace, and truth. It manifests as energy, power, guidance, insight, and influence. Light symbolizes understanding, hope, fairness, purity, and divine order. Light is a creative force. It is a source of illumination, and thus Light is a means of salvation and a doorway to Reality.

Most people have never thought of it in quite this way before, but it seems to me that every good thing human beings seek is either an inherent quality of or a direct manifestation of Light. Therefore, it would seem that what we are actually seeking is Light Itself.

And that makes sense when you consider that Light seems to be the highest non-personal spiritual concept we have come up with. The highest *personal* spiritual concept we've come up with is that of God, which most people still likely think of as some sort of personal being. And even for those who interpret the concept of God as being an impersonal being, or impersonal being *Itself*, the word *Light* seems to be a good one to describe that seemingly indescribable something we've spent ages trying to understand.

That what we are actually seeking is Light Itself also makes sense when we consider that we are all on a spiritual journey. Regardless of how "spiritual" a particular person is or is not, it remains that each one of us is engaged in a process of spiritual unfoldment.

In fact, everything we are engaged in is spiritual in nature. There is nothing actually physical or material. The mystics and quantum physicists alike will concur with me on this point. Everything we think we see is not what it appears to be. Everything we think we know is not as we believe it to be. We live in illusion.

2
Spiritual Darkness

The darkness we are discussing in this book is spiritual darkness, not physical darkness. And perhaps one easy and direct way to define this spiritual darkness would be to say that it is the polar opposite of much of what we have said about spiritual Light.

So, for instance, if Light is universal, that would make darkness limited. If Light is fundamental, that would make darkness incidental. And the concept of darkness being incidental fits in with the last sentence of the first chapter: *We live in illusion*. And that is a good way to look at spiritual darkness—as being illusion.

Whereas Light is what is, darkness is what is not appearing to be something that is. In other words, darkness is illusion which means it is a false perception or concept of reality. And a false perception or concept of reality has no substance in and of itself. It is simply a concept. So darkness is not the *opposite* of Light after all; darkness is actually the *absence* of Light. In and of itself it has no substance. Darkness is not a thing. Darkness is *no* thing. Darkness is *nothing*.

And this is actually good news. When we come to understand that darkness is merely the absence of Light, we come to understand that there is no need to concern ourselves about darkness. We don't need to fight darkness. We don't need to focus on the darkness.

We need to focus on the Light and all it encompasses. For instance, we do not need to focus on evil. We need to focus on good. By putting our attention on and thus feeding our energy into what is good, we remove our attention and our energy from what is not good. Some would say there is good and evil in the world. But it's not like that. There is good and the absence of good.

And this is a fundamental distinction that changes everything. In fact, without first making this distinction there is no hope of overcoming the darkness. The reason is that as long as we believe in darkness, we keep it in place. As long as we believe in evil, we keep it alive. Human beings give rise to darkness and evil by their attention on them and their belief in them.

And granted, there are certain things we cannot ignore, at least in the short term. An incoming punch must be dealt with. But we must begin to shift our focus from the undesirable to the desirable. Ultimately, we will overcome the undesirable by embracing the desirable. We will overcome evil by embracing good. We will overcome darkness by embracing the Light.

3
Embracing the Light

There is apparently a longstanding battle going on between good and evil. There is apparently an endless war being fought between Light and darkness. But appearances can be deceiving. In fact, *all* appearances *are* deceiving because all appearances are illusion.

For something to appear, it must take a form that can be perceived. But anything that takes form is illusion. True reality is formless. It is eternal, and it is real. Anything in form is transitory, and it is *un*real. And therein lies its weakness and our power over it.

I wrote in the first chapter that Light is a source of illumination. With illumination comes clarity and understanding. And clarity and understanding constitute enlightenment. And spiritual enlightenment is what all spiritual seekers are seeking. Yet how many are finding it? Fewer than *could* be. That's for sure.

But there is nothing standing between spiritual enlightenment and those who would seek it. Nothing real, that is. One will find what one embraces. And the truth of the matter is that most human beings embrace darkness. And what does that mean? It means they accept illusion as being real. They support illusion by their attention on it and belief in it. And they do this habitually, willingly, and without reservation.

Finding themselves in illusion, they do all they know how to do which is to deal with what they perceive in front of them as if it were really there. The average person is a slave to illusion because they know nothing else. When illusion is all you perceive, Reality is not an option. And thus, you embrace the illusion.

But it is only by embracing the Light that freedom can be attained. And what does it mean to embrace the Light? It means you turn your main focus and attention from darkness *to* Light. You look past illusion to Reality. You start to trust your inner voice over the outer noise. You make spiritual insight, understanding, and progress the main motivation in your life.

Embracing the Light is about making a fundamental change in your priorities. Whereas before you were more concerned with material matters than spiritual matters, you become more concerned with spiritual matters than with anything else. There is a battle going on between good and evil. There is a war being fought between Light and darkness. And at its core, it is a battle and a war between Reality and illusion.

4
Reality and Illusion

Light vs. darkness is just another way of saying Reality vs. illusion. Reality is what's real, and it needs only to be acknowledged to be experienced. What is illusion is unreal, and we experience it only because we acknowledge it. With illusion comes suffering. With Reality comes freedom. Spiritual freedom is the result of living in constant awareness of Reality. The Light.

So, seek not to deny or defy appearances. Instead, seek to inspect and accept that which underlies appearances. That which appears has no real substance, and thus has only the power over you that you give it. That which underlies that which appears is the only true power there is, and so by aligning yourself with that power you become a recipient of its influence.

Instead of turning *from* or running *from* something, you should be turning *toward* and running *toward* something. What? Reality. Truth. In a word, the *Light*. People are lost in darkness only because they overlook the Light. But remember, darkness is not a thing in itself. Darkness is simply the absence of Light.

So really, nothing needs to be added or taken away. Light cannot be added, because it is all that exists. Darkness cannot be taken away, because it does not exist. The truth of spiritual freedom is that it has already been attained. The only thing keeping one from knowing that is ignorance. Spiritual seekers are making spiritual finding much harder than it needs to be.

Reality is not hidden. It is only overlooked. Instead of seeing the illusion of material scarcity, see the reality of material abundance. There is no scarcity, but only the lack of abundance. Instead of seeing the illusion of physical illness, see the reality of physical health. There is no illness, but only the lack of health. It's all a matter of what you decide to see. Do you want to see something undesirable, and thus experience something undesirable? Or would you rather see something desirable, and thus experience something desirable? Scarcity or abundance? Illness or health?

The choice is yours, and it always has been. You might not have known this before, but you know it now. The endless war being fought between Light and darkness is a war in your own mind. At its core, it is a battle for your attention. There is Light, and there is darkness. And which you decide to see more of determines which will be the overriding influence in your life at any given time. And a life predominantly influenced by Light will be a life predominantly lived in Reality.

5
Living in Reality

So again, a life predominantly influenced by Light will be a life predominantly lived in Reality. Remember, Light *is* Reality. And of course, darkness is illusion.

It's quite simple, really. To live more and more in Reality, start by thinking more and more about the Light. By filling your mind with thoughts associated with Light, you will surround yourself with the frequency of Light. By surrounding yourself more and more with the frequency of Light, the vibrations of your thoughts will just naturally rise to match that frequency. And this is all conducive to living more fully in Reality.

So, you want to fill your mind with thoughts associated with Light. For starters, that means pondering the very nature of Light. Light is universal, fundamental, spiritual, divine, and good. But those are just words until you decide what those concepts mean to *you*. So, ponder them. Light is universal. Ponder just that one concept. Expect illumination to come. Then ponder concepts such as fundamental, spiritual, divine and good. Do so, and your mind will expand.

Yes, your mind will expand. It will open. Sincere, conscientious, persistent spiritual seeking and inquiry for its own sake always yields positive results over time.

Remember, Light embodies intelligence, knowledge, wisdom, grace, and truth. And by pondering the various attributes of Light, you will attract intelligence, knowledge, and wisdom. You will open the way for grace to be more a part of your life. You will understand Truth to a greater and greater degree, and thus as a natural consequence and by definition you will be living in Reality to a greater and greater degree.

Remember, Light manifests as energy, power, guidance, insight, and influence. By pondering the various attributes of Light, and thus living in Reality to a greater degree, you will have more energy and power. You will receive more inner guidance and insight. Your thoughts, feelings, and actions will be influenced by Light to a greater and greater degree.

Remember, Light symbolizes understanding, hope, fairness, purity, and divine order. Light is a creative force. It is a source of illumination, and thus Light is a means of salvation and a doorway to Reality. But what does all that *mean*? Well, it doesn't mean anything until it means something to you *personally*. And the more you ponder Light, the more it will mean to you and the more fully you will be living in Reality.

6
Contemplation

So, you want to ponder Light. In other words, you want to contemplate the concept of Light Itself as well as its various attributes and manifestations. Great. But what does it mean to contemplate something?

Contemplation is the act of thinking carefully about a particular item, event, subject, concept, or whatever. It is considering something deeply and at length, whether you are studying it, looking at it, or just thinking about it. And two key ingredients of successful *spiritual* contemplation are desire and sincerity.

The discernment and discovery of spiritual truth by way of contemplation does not come to a person unless there is a strong desire for it. Without that desire, there is really no need to go any further. And one must be sincere in their efforts to increase their understanding of spiritual concepts such as Light and Reality. Luckily, the stronger the desire for spiritual truth is, the more sincere the search for it will tend to be. Really think about these two things. *Desire* and *sincerity*. They just might be the most overlooked and underappreciated elements of successful spiritual contemplation and thus spiritual progress. Many novice "spiritual seekers" just jump right in and start studying the subject. They read and hear the thoughts of others, but they do not use critical thinking to assess the validity and value of what they read and hear.

In all their eagerness, they sacrifice some earnestness. Their desire might be strong, but their deduction is weak. They seek information, yet shun confirmation.

And where should that confirmation come from? More reading? More hearing? No. It should come from more contemplation and the intuitive spiritual knowledge that will come as a natural outcome of that contemplation. Spiritual growth is the result of enlightenment from the *inside*. Yes, spiritual study is good. It is a necessary part of the process. But any input that comes from the outside can at best only act as a catalyst to allow something to come from within.

Subjects such as ultimate spiritual truth, Light, and Reality are subjects that cannot be adequately defined in words. Words can only produce thoughts and feelings about what the words relay. But true spiritual apprehension can never be the result of only thoughts and feelings. Thoughts and feelings can do little more than to foster beliefs. But true spiritual understanding is the result of knowledge that transcends all beliefs.

7
Transcending Belief

Human life is predominantly the result of human belief. We tend to experience what we think is there. And everything we think is there is what we perceive as being there. Yet nothing we perceive with our physical senses is as we think it is, therefore we exist within a world of illusion. We exist within a world of darkness to which our senses have become accustomed. And thus, the war between Light and darkness rages on.

In the Light, there is no need for belief because true knowledge is self-evident and all-encompassing. In the darkness, there is little room for true knowledge because the objects of human belief seem so self-evident and all-encompassing. Human beings find the unknown to be extremely uncomfortable. Thus, they minimize their conscious exposure to it by substituting the beliefs they adopt for the knowledge they lack.

Thus, they end up having their beings in what amounts to a dream. They do not exist in something real and objective. They exist in something dreamlike and subjective. Material reality is an illusion, and physical human beings have hypnotized themselves into believing the illusion is something real. And that is the fundamental mistake which causes all discord.

Discord is the result of erroneous belief. When we believe things that are not true, we cannot conduct ourselves and our activities in the most prudent and productive ways because we do not have accurate information. We do not understand the true nature of ourselves, our world, our universe, and so on. Such a state of illusion and delusion cannot produce and support peace and harmony, and so discord rushes in to fill the void left by that lack of peace and harmony.

But discord can only exist in darkness. And just like the darkness within which it exists, discord itself is not a real thing. Discord is simply the lack of peace and harmony. Where peace and harmony are, discord cannot be. Peace and harmony are products of Light. And when Light shines, the nothingness of discord is nowhere to be found. It is exposed as being nothing.

This all brings us back to transcending belief. Remember, where there is true knowledge there is no need for belief; where there is belief there is little room for true knowledge. Your enlightenment must come from within, not from without. Your belief comes from your experiences which are based in illusion. So to grow, you must transcend your belief and turn within.

8
Turn Within

Although you seek far and wide for true spiritual understanding, you will not find it until you turn within. Out there you can find only information. But what is information? On the human level, information is actually nothing more than supposition based on our understanding of things that never actually happened and don't actually exist. So, assumptions pass as facts.

Again, out there you can find only information. But within, you will always find illumination. Everything perceived in the outer world—the darkness—is subject to interpretation. Everything perceived in the inner world—the Light—needs no further validation.

The spiritual journey is a journey within, and it always has been. Until one turns within, they will be going in circles. Once one turns within, they will find the path that leads straight ahead. That is all one level of it.

Another level of it is that there is actually no *out there*, thus regardless of appearances the seeker's direction is always inward. Everything on the outside is actually pointing to something on the inside. Reality shines through all illusion, as Reality is real and illusion is unreal. So seeking direction from without will in the end always provide direction that will lead within.

Thus the great benefit of spiritual teachers and spiritual teachings. They act as guideposts to help one find their way across the dark landscape of material existence. And that's one level of it. But another level of it is that because spiritual truth is all that actually exists, every sign points toward it, and every road leads to it.

That brings us back to the concept of everyone being on a spiritual journey whether they know it or not. Alive in every moment is the Light of Reality. It is always there, though it is seldom consciously discerned.

Understand that you are on a journey inward. Understand that you will find relief from your suffering to the degree you are successful moving inward. Understand that although inward is actually the only direction you can be heading, it is not until you are *purposely* and *consciously* heading in that direction that you will begin to make noticeable progress. And the more purposeful and conscious you become in your inward quest—the more you turn within—the higher the level of consciousness you will be exhibiting. And in the end and after all, it's all about consciousness because consciousness is all there is.

9
Consciousness

Any definition we could come up with for consciousness would be lacking in scope and finality. Something as far beyond human comprehension as consciousness cannot be adequately described by the human mind. Considering the many shades of meaning human beings have come up with to this point, one might well conclude that a definitive definition of consciousness is not only unlikely but impossible.

Still, the concept of consciousness is worthy of consideration by spiritual seekers. In fact, spiritual seeking is an effort to understand consciousness. Spiritual growth is a process of raising one's consciousness. Another way to put that would be to say that spiritual growth is a process of raising one's level of awareness.

The terms *consciousness* and *awareness* are sometimes used interchangeably, and there is no reason in this discussion for us to try to distinguish one from the other. Where there is consciousness, there is always awareness. And where there is awareness, there is always consciousness. You cannot have one without the other. You cannot separate one from the other. And if the human mind is indeed ill-equipped to understand consciousness, that implies that meaningful understanding of consciousness must be attained by something beyond the human mind. And just what might that something beyond the human mind be?

At the end of the last chapter, I wrote that consciousness is all there is. That implies awareness is all there is. But if consciousness is all there is, what is there for it to be conscious of other than consciousness itself? If awareness is all there is, what is there for it to be aware of other than awareness itself? Think about it.

The spiritual journey has always been one that at first takes one deeper and deeper into mind, and eventually further and further beyond mind. On the spiritual journey, one eventually discovers the Light—if only tentatively at first. And the further one journeys into Light, the more they discover that Light is all there is.

And what is Light but Reality? And what is Reality but consciousness and awareness? The process of raising one's consciousness is one that eventually reveals there is nothing to be conscious of but consciousness itself. You are not sitting on a chair right now. You are having the experience of sitting on a chair. That experience exists within consciousness as *does* the chair itself. Reality is not objective. It is totally subjective.

10
Subjective Reality

For anyone not already aware of the subjective nature of Reality, the thought of it might well seem absurd. The implications of it are mind boggling even to those who understand and subscribe to the theory. And *theory* is not really the correct word for it, at least not if you take the findings of quantum physics seriously.

Whereas in the past spirituality and science have been regarded as being distinctly different fields of study, today, thanks to quantum physics, they have come to overlap considerably. Today it is not unusual to find sincere seekers of spiritual truth reading books on quantum physics. Why? Because quantum physics is leading us to many of the same conclusions arrived at by the mystics and the various spiritual traditions.

And chief among those conclusions is that there is no such thing as objective reality. For there to be an objective reality would mean, for one thing, that it exists irrespective of any observation of it. So, for instance, this planet and the universe would exist whether or not there were any sentient beings observing it.

But the mystics have always known intuitively that reality derives its very existence from the fact that it is being observed. The quantum physicists have now discovered that the observer and the observed are not separate, and constitute two ends of the same process.

Without an observer, there is nothing to be observed. And regarding the act of observation itself, it is a subjective event that brings into being that which manifests as something observable based on how it is observed. How we see things is how they will tend to be. How we think things are is how they tend to be.

Again, and to be clear, there is no objective reality. There is no solid material reality. We are points of consciousness having our being in an endless field of consciousness. And again, and to be clear, there is nothing for consciousness to be aware of but consciousness itself. All things we perceive as having form are there *because* we perceive them. Without the perception of them, they would not and cannot exist.

And therefore, so-called material reality is totally malleable. It forms and reforms itself based on what it is perceived to be. Thus, the true power and substance is not in that which appears to be. The true power and substance is in that which perceives that which appears to be. In the end, all that is perceived to be exists in darkness, and the perceiver of it all exists in Light.

11
The Perceiver

That would seem to mean that if you are the perceiver of all you perceive, you exist in the Light and that which you perceive exists in the darkness; that would seem to mean that you exist in Reality and that which you perceive exists in illusion. That is how it would seem to be if you were the perceiver. But *are* you?

If you look in the mirror, you will see your reflection. Thus, you will perceive yourself as being you. But wait. We've determined that what is perceived exists in the darkness. Taking that at face value, it would mean that the image you see in the mirror exists in the darkness and that it is at its core actually illusion.

But if we determine that what you previously thought of as being the perceiver is in fact merely an object of perception, where does that leave *you*? And where is the actual *perceiver* of what we would have now come to recognize as being merely an *object* of *perception*? One thing is for sure. That perceiver is not *here*. That perceiver is not being reflected in the *mirror*. That perceiver is *perceiving* what is being reflected in the mirror. Think about it. We have come to understand that material reality exists in darkness. We have come to understand that material reality is an illusion. And anything that exists within that darkness and illusion is undeniably a *part* of that darkness and illusion. And the human being you think you are exists within and is thus a part of that darkness and illusion. The human being you think you are is the observed end of an observer-observed event. Think about what this *means*. You are not *perceiving*! You are being *perceived*!

Everything that takes form is illusion, because ultimate Reality cannot be confined to form. Ultimate Reality is formless. And you have form, therefore the you that you know yourself to be is not real. What is real is what is perceiving you being what you seem to be perceiving yourself being. The true perceiver is the true you. It is *that* which you seek. Yet what you seek can never be *found* because it has never been *lost*.

Don't read through the rest of this paragraph casually and jump to the next chapter without sufficiently *contemplating* what you are reading here. This is the *crux* of the whole *deal*. You are not the perceiver. You are the perceiver of you perceiving. You are not perceiving. You are being *perceived* and perceived *through*. The real you exists beyond form, and thus it exists in Reality and in the Light. Who you think you are exists in the illusion and the darkness. It is not your true self.

12
Your True Self

Light vs. darkness. Right? There is apparently an endless war being fought between Light and darkness. To understand this war, we must understand what is *at* war. On the one side there is the Light, meaning Reality, meaning your true self. On the other side is the darkness, meaning illusion, meaning your false self. Get it? You are at war with *yourself*. And who is currently winning this war between your two selves?

It goes without saying that the false self of most people is currently winning the war. Why? Because most people believe their false self is who they are. Thus, they are fully acclimated to and absorbed into the darkness meaning they are hypnotized by the illusion.

Attaining spiritual enlightenment is not so much about accomplishing something as it is about understanding that what you would seek to accomplish has already been accomplished. There is no need to overcome darkness with Light, because darkness does not exist and Light is all there is. There is no need to escape from illusion into Reality, because illusion is not real and Reality is. There is no need to rise above your false self into your true self, because you are *not* your false self and you *are* your true self. But for as long as you believe in darkness, you will remain in darkness. For as long as you believe in the illusion, you will be trapped in the illusion. For as long as you believe you are your false self, you will be bound by your false self.

But again, you are *not* your false self and so you are *not* bound. Freedom will be the result of understanding that freedom is all there is. You will gain your freedom by *being* what you are. And what *are* you? You are *Light*. You are *Reality*. You are your *true self*.

And how do you *be* Light? How do you *be* Reality? How do you *be* your true self? You live moment to moment in the realization that you are that. Know you are that, and you are that. Perceive that you are that, and you are that. And remember, you are not perceiving you are that from *here*, where you appear to be. You are perceiving you are that from *there*, where you actually are. Therefore, it is not the you that you know yourself to be that is doing the perceiving.

The you that you know yourself to be cannot perceive anything because it is not a perceiver. It is an object of perception and an instrument of perception that *seems* to think it is a perceiver of a self and world that *actually* exist in a dream. But are *you* the *dreamer*?

13
The Dreamer

Let's say that when you woke up this morning you remembered a dream, and in that dream you had swum in a lake. Would you conclude that *you* actually *swam* in a *lake*? Or would you conclude that the you that you dreamt you were was just a dream character you dreamt up to represent you, that no swimming actually occurred, and that the lake was just a dream lake?

As you can imagine, that's what most people would conclude. They would conclude that who they dreamt themselves to be did not actually do any swimming, but that they had experienced what it would be like to swim if they were the person they dreamt they were.

The mystics have always likened material life to an illusion; to a dream. If they are right, this *is* an illusion; this *is* a dream. And if you've read this far in this book, then like me you probably accept that premise as representing the truth of the matter. So, this is a dream.

And let's say you woke up from *this* dream right now. Would you conclude that *you* were just reading this book? Or would you conclude that the you that you dreamt you were was just a dream character you dreamt up to represent you, that no reading actually occurred, and that the book was just a dream book?

Get it? This life, this world, everything you think you see, know, and experience—it's all just part of a dream. And as disconcerting a concept as this might seem to be, *you* are *not* the *dreamer*. You are merely a *dream character* within the dreamer's dream. See?

The you that you have always thought yourself to be—your false self—is just a dream character. The you that you actually are—your true self—is the real dreamer. *You* as *you* do not exist. Not in the Light; not in Reality. You as you exist only in the darkness; only in the illusion. You in form are nowhere. You beyond form are in the only place anything could be—everywhere.

Light is dreaming a dream of darkness. Reality is dreaming a dream of illusion. Your true self is dreaming a dream of your false self. Life is truly but a dream.

And where is this dream leading us? It is leading us nowhere, because there is nowhere for us to go. Then where are we now? We are nowhere, because there is nowhere for us to be. Even if there was somewhere for us to be, we don't exist so we couldn't be there. In form, we are in illusion. Beyond form, we are in Light.

14
Beyond Form

There is apparently an endless war being fought between Light and darkness. To understand this war, we must understand what is *at* war. On the one side there is the Light, meaning Reality, meaning your true self, meaning *formlessness*. On the other side is the darkness, meaning illusion, meaning your false self, meaning *form*. And the only way to win the war between formlessness and form is to go *beyond form*.

And going beyond form is an act of perception. When we perceive clearly, we see beyond the darkness, the illusion, and the false self. The key to making this work is reminding ourselves that it is not our false self that is doing the perceiving, but that it is our true self.

There is apparently an endless war being fought between Light and darkness. But it is not *really* being fought. It is only *apparently* being fought. The darkness is nothing. So how could something that is *nothing* fight *anything*, much less *everything*? And the Light is everything. So how could something that is *everything* fight *anything*, much less *nothing*?

The Light we have discussed in this book is spiritual Light, not physical light. Trying to fit spiritual Light into physical words can be likened to, say, trying to stuff the sun into your pocket. Try as you might, you're just not going to be able to do it. But I did what I could.

The darkness we have discussed in this book is spiritual darkness, not physical darkness. And we have come to understand this darkness to be nothing more than the absence of Light. Darkness is mere illusion.

There is apparently an endless war being fought between Light and darkness. But appearances can be deceiving. In fact, *all* appearances *are* deceiving because all appearances are illusion. And what is an appearance other than something in apparent form?

All things we perceive as having form are there *because* we perceive them. Without the perception of them, they do not and cannot exist. And therefore, so-called material reality is totally malleable. It forms and reforms itself based on what it is perceived to be.

The endless war being fought between Light and darkness is a war in your own mind. At its core, it is a battle for your attention. Light or darkness? Which you see more of determines which will be the overriding influence in your life. And a life predominantly influenced by Light will be a life predominantly lived in Reality.

AFTERWORD

Thank you for reading this book. I hope you have enjoyed it. And I hope you will continue to benefit from having read it. I have benefited greatly from having read countless books over the years.

I began to find my first self-help, spiritual, and metaphysical books in my early twenties, not long after I moved from New Jersey to California to try to find my way in the world. Before that move, I had no idea such books even existed.

And honestly, were it not for such books and my intense desire to learn, to grow, and to improve myself and my circumstances, I would have gone down a completely different road in life—a road I would rather not even think about or imagine.

Who could deny the assertion that books can and do change lives? It is my mission to write some of those books that do indeed change lives. I want people's lives to be better because I lived and because I wrote.

There are reasons I came into this life, and writing is one of them. I am living the life I was meant to live, and it is my sincere desire that you will live the life you were meant to live.

Can I ask two favors of you? First, if you think this or any of my other books can help people in some of the

Afterword

ways they could use help, will you help spread the word about me and my writings? You could do that by loaning my books to others, giving my books as gifts, and by telling people about my books and about me. By doing these things, you will bless me beyond measure, and I truly believe you will bless others beyond measure as well.

Second, please consider writing an honest review for this book. Doing so will help other readers decide whether or not the book might be right for them. And keep in mind that a review does not have to be long. Even just a few words or a sentence or two could be sufficient. And if you do not feel inclined to write a review at all, you can simply click on a star rating to rate the book and still have your voice heard.

Finally, always remember, you are capable of so much more than you have ever imagined. Learn, believe, act, and persist. Do those four things, and nothing will stop you from continuing to build a better and better life for yourself and for those you care about.

Peace & Plenty . . .

ABOUT THE AUTHOR

James Goi Jr., aka The Attract Money Guru™, is the bestselling author of the internationally published *How to Attract Money Using Mind Power*, a book that set a new standard for concise, no-nonsense, straight-to-the-point self-help books. First published in 2007, that game-changing book continues to transform lives around the world. And though it would be years before James would write new books, and even more years before he would publish new books, that first book set the tone for his writing career. The tagline for James as an author and publisher is Books to Awaken, Uplift, and Empower™. And James takes those words seriously, as is evident in every book he writes. James: is a relative recluse and spends most of his time alone; is an advanced mind-power practitioner, a natural-born astral traveler, and an experienced lucid dreamer; has had life-changing encounters with both angels and demons, and even sees some dead people; has been the grateful recipient of an inordinate amount of lifesaving divine intervention; is a poet and songwriter; is a genuinely nice guy who cares about people and all forms of life; fasts regularly; is a sincere seeker of higher human health; is an objective observer, a persistent ponderer, and a deliberate deducer; and has a supple sense of heady humor.

STAY IN TOUCH WITH JAMES

If you are a sincere seeker of spiritual truth and/or a determined pursuer of material wealth and success, James could be the lifeline and the go-to resource you have been hoping to find. Step One, subscribe to James's free monthly *Mind Power & Money Ezine* here: jamesgoijr.com/subscriber-page.html. Step Two, connect with James online anywhere and everywhere you can find him. You can start here:

Facebook.com/JamesGoiJr
Facebook.com/JamesGoiJrPublicPage
Facbook.com/HowToAttractMoneyUsingMindPower
Twitter.com/JamesGoiJr
Linkedin.com/in/JamesGoiJr
Pinterest.com/JamesGoiJr
Youtube.com/JamesGoiJr
Instagram.com/JamesGoiJr
Goodreads.com/JamesGoiJr
jamesgoijr.tumblr.com

James' Amazon Author Page

A great resource to help you keep abreast of James's ever-expanding list of books is his author page at Amazon.com. There you will find all of his published writings and have easy access to them in the various editions in which they will be published.

Suggested for You

From time to time, James comes across products he thinks might be of interest to his readers, and he posts the links to those products on his website. To see what might be currently listed, visit that page here: jamesgoijr.com/suggested.html

SPECIAL ACKNOWLEDGEMENT

To Kathy Darlene Hunt, who has been my rock, my Light, my safety net, and my buffer since I was in my twenties. She rightfully shares in the credit for every book I've written, for the books I'm working on now, and for every single book I will ever write.

Kathy Darlene Hunt
Author of *A Child of the Light*
jamesgoijr.com/kdh.html

A FREE GIFT FOR YOU!

Attract Money Forever will deepen your understanding of metaphysics and mind-power principles as they relate to attracting money, manifesting abundance, and governing material reality. You'll learn how to use time-tested, time-honored, practical, and spiritual techniques to be more prosperous and improve your life in astounding and meaningful ways. Visit jamesgoijr.com/subscriber-page.html for your free download copy of this amazing book and to receive James's free monthly *Mind Power & Money Ezine*.

FURTHER READING

The 80/20 Principle by Richard Koch
The ABCs of Success by Bob Proctor
Abundance Now by Lisa Nichols and Janet Switzer
Act Like a Success, Think Like a Success by Steve Harvey
The Amazing Power of Deliberate Intent by Esther Hicks and Jerry Hicks
As a Man Thinketh by James Allen
Awakened Imagination by Neville Goddard
The Awakened Millionaire by Joe Vitale
Awaken the Giant Within by Tony Robbins
Being and Vibration by Joseph Rael with Mary Elizabeth Marlow
The Biology of Belief by Bruce H. Lipton, Ph.D.
Breaking the Habit of Being Yourself by Dr. Joe Dispenza
The Charge by Brendon Burchard
Choice Point by Harry Massey and David R. Hamilton, Ph.D.
Clarity by Jamie Smart
The Compound Effect by Darren Hardy
The Cosmic Code by Heinz R. Pagels
The Cosmic Ordering Service by Barbel Mohr
The Council of Light by Danielle Rama Hoffman
Create Your Own Future by Brian Tracy
Creating on Purpose by Anodea Judith and Lion Goodman
Creative Visualization by Shakti Gawain
The Dancing Wu Li Masters by Gary Zukav
The Diamond in Your Pocket by Gangaji
The Dice Game of Shiva by Richard Smoley
Divine Audacity by Linda Martella-Whitsett
The Divine Matrix by Gregg Braden

Further Reading

Dreamed Up Reality by Dr. Bernardo Kastrup
The Dynamic Laws of Prosperity by Catherine Ponder
Emergence by Derek Rydall
The Field by Lynne McTaggart
Follow Your Passion, Find Your Power by Bob Doyle
The Four Desires by Rod Stryker
Frequency by Penney Peirce
The Game of Life and How to Play It by Florence Scovel Shinn
Having It All by John Assaraf
The Hidden Power by Thomas Troward
How Consciousness Commands Matter by Dr. Larry Farwell
How Successful People Think by John C. Maxwell
I AM by Vivian E. Amis
I Wish I Knew This 20 Years Ago by Justin Perry
Infinite Potential by Lothar Schafer
Instant Motivation by Chantal Burns
It Works by RHJ
Jack Canfield's Key to Living the Law of Attraction by Jack Canfield and D.D. Watkins
Just Ask the Universe by Michael Samuels
Key to Yourself by Venice J. Bloodworth
The Law of Agreement by Tony Burroghs
Lessons in Truth by H. Emilie Cady
Life Power and How to Use It by Elizabeth Towne
Life Visioning by Michael Bernard Beckwith
Live Your Dreams by Les Brown
The Lost Writings of Wu Hsin by Wu Hsin and Roy Melvyn (Translator)
The Magical Approach by Seth, Jane Roberts, and Robert F. Butts
The Magic Lamp by Keith Ellis
The Magic of Believing by Claude M. Bristol
The Magic of Thinking Big by David J. Schwartz

Further Reading

Make Magic of Your Life by T. Thorne Coyle
Manifesting Change by Mike Dooley
The Map by Boni Lonnsburry
The Master Key System by Charles F. Haanel
The Millionaire Mind by Thomas J. Stanley
Mind and Success by W. Ellis Williams
Mind into Matter by Fred Alan Wolf, Ph.D.
Mind Power into the 21st Century by John Kehoe
Miracles by Stuart Wilde
The Miracles in You by Mark Victor Hansen and Ben Carson (Foreword)
Mysticism and the New Physics by Michael Talbot
New Physics and the Mind by Robert Paster
The One Command by Asara Lovejoy
One Mind by Larry Dossey, M.D.
The One Thing by Garry Keller with Jay Papasan
One Simple Idea by Mitch Horowitz
Our Invisible Supply by Frances Larimer Warner
Our Wishes Fulfilled by Dr. Wayne W. Dyer
Physics on the Fringe by Margaret Wertheim
Playing the Quantum Field by Brenda Anderson
The Power of Now by Eckhart Tolle
The Power of Positive Thinking by Dr. Norman Vincent Peale
The Power of Your Subconscious Mind by Joseph Murphy
The Power to Get Things Done by Steve Levinson Ph.D. and Chris Cooper
Programming the Universe by Seth Lloyd
Prosperity by Charles Fillmore
Psycho-Cybernetics by Maxwell Maltz
Quantum Creativity by Pamela Meyer
Quantum Jumps by Cynthia Sue Larson
Quantum Reality by Nick Herbert
The Quantum Self by Danah Zohar
Reality Unveiled by Ziad Masri

Further Reading

Reality Creation 101 by Christopher A. Pinckley
The Sacred Six by JB Glossinger
The School of Greatness by Lewis Howes
The Science of Getting Rich by Wallace D. Wattles
The Science of Mind by Ernest Holmes
The Secret by Rhonda Byrne
The Secret of the Ages by Robert Collier
The Self-Aware Universe by Amit Goswami
Shadows of the Mind by Roger Penrose
Shift Your Mind by Steve Chandler
The Slight Edge by Jeff Olson
Soul Purpose by Mark Thurstan, Ph.D.
Spiritual Economics by Eric Butterworth
Supreme Influence by Niurka
There Are No Accidents by Robert E. Hopcke
Think and Grow Rich by Napoleon Hill
Thought Power by Annie Besant
Thoughts Are Things by Prentice Mulford
True Purpose by Tim Kelley
True Spirituality & the Law of Attraction by Karl W. Gruber
The Universe Is a Dream by Alexander Marchand
Unleash Your Full Potential by James Rick
Warped Passages by Lisa Randall
The Way of Liberation by Adyashanti
What Is Self? by Bernadette Roberts
The Wisdom Within by Dr. Irving Oyle and Susan Jean
Within the Power of Universal Mind by Rochelle Sparrow and Courtney Kane
Working with the Law by Raymond Holliwell
You Are the Universe by Deepak Chopra and Menas C. Kafatos
You Are the World by Jiddu Krishnamurti
Your Invisible Power by Genevieve Behrend
You Unlimited by Norman S. Lunde
The Zigzag Principle by Rich Christiansen

Made in United States
Orlando, FL
11 July 2023